The Story of

Seaside Holidays

Monica Hughes

www.raintreepublishers.co.uk
Visit our website to find out more information about **Raintree** books.

To order:
☎ Phone 44 (0) 1865 888112
🖹 Send a fax to 44 (0) 1865 314091
🖥 Visit the Raintree Bookshop at **www.raintreepublishers.co.uk** to browse our catalogue and order online.

First published in Great Britain by Raintree, Halley Court, Jordan Hill, Oxford OX2 8EJ, part of Pearson Education. Raintree is a registered trademark of Pearson Education Ltd.

Editorial: Sian Smith
Design: Kimberley R. Miracle, Big Top and Joanna Hinton-Malivoire
Picture research: Ruth Blair
Production: Duncan Gilbert
Illustrated by Beehive Illustration
Originated by Dot Gradations

Printed and bound in China by Leo Paper Group

ISBN 978 1 4062 1007 1 (hardback)
ISBN 978 1 4062 1017 0 (paperback)

12 11 10 09
10 9 8 7 6 5 4 3 2

British Library Cataloguing in Publication Data
Hughes, Monica
   The story of seaside holidays
1. Seaside resorts - History - Juvenile literature
2. Vacations - History - Juvenile literature
3. Seaside resorts - Juvenile literature
4. Vacations - Juvenile literature
   I. Title

306.4'8125'09

Acknowledgments
The publishers would like to thank the following for permission to reproduce photographs: ©Alamy pp.7 (Ilan Rosen), 5 (Imagestate); ©Corbis pp. 12, 13 (Bettmann), 9 (Bo Zaunders), 6, 11 (Hulton-Deutsch Collection); ©istockphoto.com pp.11, 13, 17; ©Pearson Education Ltd pp.12 (Debbie Rowe), 12 (Malcolm Harris); ©photolibrary.com pp.11 (Arcangel Images), 8, 14, 16, 18 (Frances Frith Collection), 19 (Johner), 15 (Robert Harding Travel), 4, 10 (Voller Ernst); ©Superstock p.11.

Cover photograph reproduced with permission of ©Topham Picturepoint.

Every effort has been made to contact copyright holders of any material reproduced in this book. Any omissions will be rectified in subsequent printings if notice is given to the publisher.

Contents

Some words are printed in bold, **like this**. You can find out what they mean in the glossary.

Holiday or holy day

A seaside holiday over one hundred years ago.

The word holiday comes from two words 'holy' and 'day'. Long ago people were only allowed to stop work for **religious festivals** such as Christmas and Easter. This was called a holiday. We still have holidays at these times today. But now we also take other holidays throughout the year.

A family enjoying a seaside holiday today.

Most seaside holidays take place in the summer months. For more than two hundred years people have visited the seaside to enjoy the beach. Holidays are a time to relax, have fun, and try new things.

Getting to the seaside

Trains were busy as lots of people wanted to go to the seaside.

More than one hundred years ago, Queen Victoria was queen of Britain. People who lived at that time are called **Victorians**. In Victorian times people went on holiday to the seaside by steam train.

Today people can still go to the seaside by train, but they can also travel there in other ways. They can drive there in couches or cars. People can also visit the seaside in other countries by aeroplane.

Staying at the seaside

hotels

The seafront at Teignmouth one hundred years ago.

Long ago only rich children went on holiday for two weeks. They stayed in large hotels by the beach. Poorer children only had a day trip to the seaside.

hotels

The seafront at Brighton today.

Now, many people go on holiday for two weeks. Lots of families still stay in hotels or in **apartments** near the beach. Camping in tents or staying in caravans is also popular.

Food at the seaside

A Victorian picnic on the beach.

Victorian children liked the relaxed way of eating at the seaside. They could buy food from beach **stalls** and eat it straight away. Many families liked to have picnics on the seafront or on the beach. This still happens today.

Sticks of rock, candy floss, and ice cream have all been eaten at the seaside for more than a hundred years.

For many years people have also enjoyed eating **seafood** such as shrimps, cockles, and whelks by the sea. Fish and chips has always been a favourite seaside food.

Clothes at the seaside

swimming costume.

Victorian clothes.

Clothes today.

The clothes people wear on the beach have changed over time. **Victorians** liked to keep their bodies covered up. They wore their normal clothes to the beach. Today people often wear shorter clothes, such as T-shirts and shorts.

Ladies wore swimming costumes like this about one hundred years ago.

Swimming costumes today.

Swimming costumes have also changed. Victorian ladies wore costumes that covered their shoulders and legs. Today swimming costumes are much shorter and come in many different colours.

On the beach and in the sea

Donkey rides at Rhyl,
one hundred years ago.

Children have always had fun playing on the beach. Long ago they used spades and metal buckets to make sandcastles. Today buckets and spades are made from plastic.

For more than a hundred years children have watched Punch and Judy shows and enjoyed donkey rides on the beach. Sometimes you can still find these at the seaside today.

People enjoying the sea
and the beach today.

Most **Victorian** children could not swim.
They **paddled** in the sea. Now most
children have fun swimming in the sea and
playing in the waves. People also like surfing,
windsurfing, and boating.

On the promenade and the pier

The promenade in Scarborough one hundred years ago.

Long ago families walked along the **promenade**. This is the path along the seafront. Here they listened to a band or relaxed in deckchairs. There were also funfairs and merry-go-rounds.

Today, people still like to walk along the prom. They also still enjoy visiting funfairs, where they can go on big roller coasters and other fun rides.

This is the arcade on Brighton pier today.

Piers were important in **Victorian** times because they were places where boats could drop off passengers. Some piers had small shops called **kiosks** selling **souvenirs**, such as sticks of rock. Some had **amusement arcades** where people could play games. Large piers at the seaside today still have arcades and shops where people can buy souvenirs.

Holidays then and now

Seaside holidays in Hastings about one hundred years ago.

Long ago people often went to a beach close to where they lived for their holidays. Today many families go on seaside holidays in other countries. Now it is much easier for people to travel all over the world.

A seaside holiday in another country today.

Seaside holidays in this country have become less **popular**. Some seaside towns are hardly visited these days. Have you ever been to the seaside? How do you think your holiday was different from seaside holidays in the past?

Teachers' guide

These books have followed the QCA guidelines closely, but space has not allowed us to cover all the information and vocabulary the QCA suggest. Any suggested material not covered in the book is added to the discussion points below. The books can simply be read as information books, or they could be used as a focus for studying the unit. Below are discussion points grouped in pairs of pages, with suggested follow-up activities.

Please read the For use with this book section at the end of these pages.

PAGES 4–5

Talk about:
- Discuss the link between 'holy day' and 'holiday'. Explain that when there were holy days, almost everyone in Britain was Christian and being a Catholic was the only Christian religion. What 'holy days' do we have holidays around now? Why are they much less about religion now for many people?

Possible activity:
- Make a class timeline for a year, marking on it the school holidays.
- Mark where they have been on holiday on a map.

PAGES 6–7

Talk about:
- Discuss going to the seaside and why people might want to go there for a holiday. Talk about how the class have travelled to go on holiday. Discuss when these types of transport came into use and if their parents/carers, grandparents might have used them. Explain the types of transport the Victorians could use to go on holiday. Say transport is one clue to sort which of the two photos is modern and which is older.

Possible activity:
- Brainstorm other kinds of clues from the picture: clothes, hairstyles, etc.
- Sort various pictures of seaside holidays into sets of modern, recent, older, oldest.

PAGES 8–9

Talk about:
- Discuss the factors that affect where you go on holiday: the time off you have, the cost of the holiday, various likes and dislikes to do with where to stay (do you hate camping?) and what to do (do you like walking holidays?) and also, what is available (even if you had huge amounts of money, it would not be possible to go to the moon on holiday today).

Possible activity:
- Make a simple causation spider diagram of the various factors that affect the kind of holiday a person takes.

PAGES 10–11

Talk about:
- Discuss the children's experience of holiday food. Is there anything that they only eat on holiday? Many people in Victorian times only ate ice cream on holiday – they had no fridges or freezers. Discuss the similarities and differences between the various images of beach picnics that you have collected (see For use with this book section).

Possible activity:
- Make a chart showing similarities and differences between the beach picnic on page 11 and the one(s) you have found.

PAGES 12–13

Talk about:
- Discuss the fact that it was not only how many clothes people wore, but what they were made of that was different in the past. This would be a good chance for children to interview their relatives or neighbours about their holidays and ask about what they wore on the beach and swimsuits – older people may remember wearing knitted wool swimsuits, for example, others might remember the first bikinis.

Possible activity:
- Compile a series of questions to ask a relative/neighbour who has had a seaside holiday (when, where, who with, what did they wear/eat/do). Did they listen to music and, if so, how?)

PAGES 14–15

Talk about:
- Compare the images on pages 4–5 and discuss buckets and spades today and in the past.
- Discuss beach activities and how they are affected by age, size, skill (babies can't sit on a donkey unaided – huge numbers of adults can't windsurf). Some skills run in families, because they become a family activity (for example, swimming).

Possible activity:
- Survey how many children in the class can swim and of who in their family can swim. Does swimming run in families in this class?

PAGES 16–17

Talk about:
- Discuss the idea of listening to a band playing on the prom. How would people listen to music on the beach now? How did their relatives/neighbours listen to music? Discuss the fact that many funfairs in seaside towns have become run down – they can't compete with places like Alton Towers. Many Victorian piers were not repaired and some have blown down in storms and not been replaced.

Possible activity:
- Find as many activities as possible in the photo file. Make a frequency chart.

PAGES 18–19

Talk about:
- What have we learned about seaside holidays? What things have stayed the same and what is different? What most affects the kinds of holidays people take?

Possible activity:
- Make a display about seaside holidays now, for parents/carers/grandparents/the Victorians, using all the evidence they have collected.
- Make a poster for their favourite holiday.

For use with this book

It would be useful if you could collect modern pictures of beach picnics and seaside holidays and also some from previous decades. Because of the National Curriculum requirements, there are many books available on this from libraries and many images on line.

QCA advise a visit from a older person to the class to talk about their seaside holidays.

Find out more

Books

Life in the Past: Victorian Seaside Holidays, Mandy Ross (Heinemann Library, 2004)

Things To Do At the Seaside, Paul Humphrey (Franklin Watts, 2007)

What is it Like Now? At the Seaside, Tony Pickford (Heinemann Library, 2003)

What Was It Like in the Past? At the Seaside, Louise and Richard Spilsbury (Heinemann Library, 2003)

A Victorian Child Goes to the Seaside, Christine Butterwort (Heinemann, 2002)

Websites

www.nationaltrust.org.uk
The National Trust protects and owns many beautiful places around the coast so that everyone can use and enjoy them.

www.museumofchildhood.org.uk
This museum in London has displays about many aspects of childhood.

www.rspb.org.uk/youth/
The Royal Society for the Protection of Birds looks after some seaside places. You can find out about their children's clubs and activities at this website.

Glossary

amusement arcade area with coin-operated machines and games

apartment room or rooms in a building

kiosk small shop

paddle walk bare foot in water

pier long platform that is built over the sea for people to walk on. Boats can drop off their passengers on piers.

popular liked by many people

promenade (or prom) wide path for people to walk along. At the seaside this path is usually next to the sea.

religious festivals holy celebration

seafood food that comes from the sea, for example, fish

souvenir something you buy that reminds you of your holiday

stall table or small shop where things can be bought

Victorian from the time of Queen Victoria. This was more than one hundred years ago.

Index